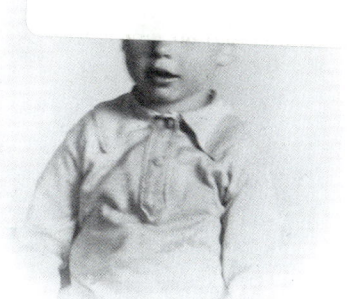

A CHILD'S DYLAN THOMAS

Phil Carradice

Pont

First published in 2014 by Pont Books, an imprint of
Gomer Press, Llandysul, Ceredigion, SA44 4JL

ISBN 978 1 84851 749 3

A CIP record for this title is available from the British Library.

© Copyright text: Phil Carradice, 2014
© Copyright photographs as noted below, 2014

Phil Carradice has asserted his moral right under the
Copyright, Designs and Patents Act, 1988
to be identified as author of this work.

All rights reserved. No part of this book may be reproduced,
stored in a retrieval system, or transmitted in any form
or by any means, electronic, electrostatic, magnetic tape, mechanical,
photocopying, recording or otherwise without permission
in writing from the above publishers.

This book is published with the financial support of the
Welsh Books Council.

Printed and bound in Wales at
Gomer Press, Llandysul, Ceredigion

Acknowledgements

The publishers wish to thank the following for granting permission to use the photographs on these pages:

BBC Cymru: 12
Carmarthenshire County Council: 13, 22, 23 (and back cover)
Trudy Carradice: 28, 32
Sian Davies: 21
South Wales Evening Post: 19, 20
West Glamorgan Archive Service: 8, 14, 15
City and County of Swansea, Economic Development Department: 32
Rebecca Griffith: 2, 4, 10i, 11, 26, 27, 29
Anne and Geoff Haden: 4
Viv Sayer: 7, 10ii, 16, 18, 24
Jeff Towns/Dylan's Bookstore Collection: 5, 6i (and front cover), ii, 17, 25
Nora Summers/Jeff Towns Dylan's Bookstore Collection: 17
Welsh Arts Council & Sue Shields: 30

'To begin at the beginning...'

Dylan Thomas knew, almost from the moment he learned to walk and talk, what he wanted to be when he grew up. He wanted to be a writer and, in particular, he wanted to be a poet.

He loved words: hearing them, reading them and speaking them. Above all, he loved writing them. To him, words were like paint and he used them to colour his poems and stories, creating wonderful pictures in a way that very few people had imagined possible. His descriptions of childhood in Swansea and his days at Fern Hill are some of the most magical ever written.

Dylan Marlais Thomas was born on 27 October 1914 at 5 Cwmdonkin Drive in the Uplands area of Swansea.

The name Dylan was very unusual. It was chosen by his father, David John (DJ) Thomas, because it was the name of a character in a story from the *Mabinogi*, the ancient folk tales of Wales. 'Marlais' was based on the name of a great-uncle who had been a well-known poet and preacher.

Dylan was rather a spoiled child, mollycoddled by his mother, Florence. At the first hint of a cold or sniffle, she would tuck him up in bed and feed him sweets, or squares of bread coated in sugar and milk. Going to bed and claiming to be ill became an easy way of dealing with problems; it was something Dylan did even as a grown-up.

Florence Thomas, the writer's mother

Florence was so protective of her son that he didn't go to school until he was seven years old. Dylan seems to have enjoyed his time at his first school in Mirador Crescent in the Uplands, where he later remembered making the worst raffia dollies and putting water in another child's galoshes (wellingtons)!

D. J. Thomas

Dylan's father was strict. He was an English teacher at Swansea Grammar School and had wanted to be a writer. Now he was ambitious for his son. When Dylan was a baby, instead of singing him nursery rhymes, he read to him from Shakespeare and the Bible. Dylan didn't know what the words meant, but he loved the sound of them.

When he was growing up, Dylan was surrounded by books, and when he started to write, his father would 'mark' his work, praising what he liked but using red pen to show what he didn't.

All writers need a 'critical friend' but DJ's criticism could be very sharp!

As far as DJ was concerned, English was the best language if you wanted to get ahead. So the young Dylan was brought up to speak only English even though both his parents were Welsh speakers from west Wales.

Dylan loved the company of their brothers and sisters, especially at Christmas. You can read about his aunts and uncles in *A Child's Christmas in Wales* (available these days in Welsh too!).

He also enjoyed visiting his Aunty Ann and Uncle Jack at their farm, Fern Hill, near Llansteffan.

Fern Hill Farm, near Llansteffan, Carmarthenshire

Cwmdonkin Park when Dylan was a small child

From an early age, places and people were important to Dylan. He played in Cwmdonkin Park near his home. He had the knack of making friends and, even though he was sometimes thoughtless and unkind, he built up a wide circle of playmates.

As he grew older, Dylan got a reputation for being a bit of a bad boy. He would steal sweets from the local sweet shop and then lie back on the seats of the Uplands Cinema, happily puffing at cigarettes or cigars. Telling fibs was as easy as breathing. He wrote in one of his stories how he frightened his mother by cutting his knee with a penknife, putting the blood on his handkerchief and saying that it had come out of his ears.

Although Cwmdonkin Park was where Dylan's imagination took flight, he travelled further afield, to Mumbles and the Gower peninsula west of Swansea, as well as to the Carmarthenshire coast beyond. He never forgot the beauty of these places which found their way into his short stories.

Cwmdonkin Park

Llansteffan in Carmarthenshire, featured in *A Visit to Grandpa*

Rhossili Bay, Gower

Just before his eleventh birthday, Dylan started at Swansea Grammar School. He did not like school very much and the only subject he was any good at was English. He wrote poems and comic essays for the school magazine and went on to be its editor in his final year.

The only other thing he enjoyed at school was long-distance running. Until the day he died, he kept a newpaper article in his pocket about how he'd won the school mile race.

He wrote a story, 'Extraordinary Little Cough', about a camping trip to Gower where one of the characters runs the whole length of Rhossili beach without stopping. Nearly all of the story details – the tents, the school bullies, the run along the sand – were based on things that had really happened in his life.

Whilst at grammar school, Dylan appeared in several plays. He acted the part of Oliver Cromwell in one. Even then it was his rich, deep voice that caught people's attention.

At Warmley, the house of schoolmate Daniel Jones who later became a composer, he and his friend set up some loudspeakers and began broadcasting. They called it the Warmley Broadcasting Corporation. Dylan read his poems 'over the air' for the first time. This was great practice for his later career as a radio broadcaster.

Dylan Thomas broadcasting with the BBC

Dylan as a young man

When he was sixteen, Dylan Marlais Thomas left school and began working as a reporter on the local paper, the *South Wales Echo*. He wasn't very good at it and the only thing he liked about the job was swaggering around the town, coat collar turned up, and hat at a jaunty angle over his eyes.

Dylan lasted only eighteen months as a reporter. Apart from a short period as a script writer, it was the only full-time job he ever had. From now on he would earn his living as a writer, sitting in his bedroom or in the Kardomah cafe in Swansea.

It wasn't long before Dylan was having his work accepted by poetry magazines.

When he won a prize to have a book of his poems published, he called it *Eighteen Poems*. Although it wasn't a bestseller, it did well enough to keep editors and publishers interested in the young writer from Wales.

But Dylan had started to feel stifled by his life in Swansea and was eager to get away. Perhaps he didn't realise that Wales, its people and its landscape, were important to his writing. He could not write properly anywhere else.

Dylan made many visits to London but spent more time in the city pubs than he ever did writing. He was always drawn back to the Swansea he claimed to hate; he needed the familiar streets and the people he knew so well to be able to write.

When he was in London he liked to play the part of the way-out artist. He did this in Swansea too.

One of his favourite games was running about on all fours, pretending to be a dog. Once, outside a pub in the Mumbles, he bit an iron lamp-post while playing this game and chipped his front tooth!

The Mermaid Hotel, Mumbles, one of Dylan's favourite haunts

It was during this time that Dylan got the reputation of being a wild, drunken poet. People still talk about his behaviour. They may never have read a word he wrote but everyone knows about his antics and about his stormy relationship with Caitlin Macnamara.

Dylan Thomas was in a pub in London when he met his future wife. Caitlin was with the Welsh artist Augustus John. Dylan followed them all the way to the picturesque seaside town of Laugharne, where Augustus John decided he had finally had enough. There was a brawl in a pub car park and Dylan, who was no good at fighting, ended up lying in the dust.

The seaside town of Laugharne

Dylan and Caitlin Thomas

To everyone's surprise, it wasn't long before Dylan and Caitlin got married. Perhaps he thought she was going to take care of him but Caitlin was a strong personality – and she could fight better than Dylan, too.

But she believed in his work and was determined that he should not waste his talent.

Sea View, Laugharne

After they were married, Dylan and Caitlin settled in Laugharne in a house called Sea View.

The critics and the public loved Dylan's work but he seemed unable to make his money last. And Caitlin was just as bad. The two of them were always short of money and used to quarrel about it. They often ate cockles that Caitlin collected from the estuary.

It was at this time that Dylan wrote a collection of stories about his childhood and the Swansea days, *Portrait of the Artist as a Young Dog*. His work was full of memories and often very funny.

But still Dylan hankered after London.

When war broke out in 1939, Dylan was pleased when he was declared physically unfit to join the army. He did not like the idea of carrying a gun.

He spent the war in a number of different places, including London, Oxford and Swansea, writing film scripts for the Ministry of Information.

In February 1941 Swansea was heavily bombed. The 'three nights' blitz' destroyed much of the town that Dylan knew and loved.

Swansea in ruins

Dylan was very upset by the destruction of Swansea, his 'ugly, lovely town'. He wrote 'Return Journey' for a BBC radio broadcast. It is very moving because in it he records his feelings of loss.

In the broadcast an old park keeper recounts all the things the young Dylan got up to in Cwmdonkin Park. He finishes by saying, 'I think he was happy all the time.' That happy time had gone for ever, as flattened and lifeless as the bombed-out streets of Swansea.

In the final years of the war Dylan and Caitlin lived in New Quay in Ceredigion and it was there that he first had the idea for a radio play. In a world that had clearly gone mad, the only place to be was a community that was equally crazy. *The Town that was Mad* was the working title for a play for voices that eventually became *Under Milk Wood*.

The town in the play is probably made up of a combination of places – Laugharne, Llansteffan and New Quay amongst them.

New Quay, Ceredigion

The Boathouse, Laugharne

When peace came in 1945, Dylan was restless. Although he was doing more and more work for the BBC, presenting programmes and reading specially written scripts, he was not really doing what he wanted to do – write poetry.

Then, in 1949, a wealthy friend, Margaret Taylor, bought the Boathouse in Laugharne and gave it to Dylan and Caitlin. It was an old, run-down place but it was their first real home and they moved into their new house in the early summer.

Inside Dylan's writing shed

Immediately, Dylan began to write again, using an old shed standing alongside the path that led from the town to the Boathouse, as a study. The views out over the estuary were magnificent – Dylan could not fail to be inspired. He was back in Wales and he could be creative once more.

Brown's Hotel, Laugharne, where Dylan was a 'regular'

Soon after Dylan and Caitlin moved into the Boathouse, there came an invitation to go to America to read his work aloud and give talks. To Dylan, it seemed that this could be the answer to all his money worries. Starting in 1950, he made four trips to the United States.

The reading tours were hugely successful, thousands hanging spellbound on his every word. Dylan was well paid for his work but, unfortunately, he spent the money almost as quickly as he earned it.

In New York, he was a regular visitor to the bars and taverns. Everyone loved the wild Welsh poet but the long hours of drinking and party-going put a terrible strain on his health.

Travelling around America meant that it was impossible for Dylan to write. For that, he would have to wait until he returned to Wales.

Back home, Dylan found that his father was seriously ill, and did not have long to live. He responded by writing 'Do Not Go Gentle Into That Good Night', begging his father to fight against his coming death. Many people think that it's Dylan's greatest poem.

At the same time that he was grieving for his father, Dylan was working hard on *Under Milk Wood*. Perhaps creating the eccentric world of Llareggub and revelling in the magic of words helped him push away his sadness. He was still working on the play till just before the first performance in America in May 1953.

At home Dylan was earning a lot of money from his writing but he still had many debts, and local tradesmen were, quite literally, hammering on the door. And so he decided to go back to America in the autumn, leaving Caitlin in Laugharne with their three children.

Under Milk Wood is set at a time when it was important to seem respectable. The play made people laugh because, behind the lace curtains of a 'well-behaved' Welsh town, every kind of mischief is happening.

Mr Pugh the schoolteacher takes his wife a cup of tea in bed, muttering what he'd really like to do: put poison in her tea, put weedkiller in her biscuit, throttle the parakeet and spit in the vases!

Dylan must have enjoyed creating the cast of crazy characters: Mr Organ Morgan who loves music (though his wife hates it), or blind Captain Cat who sits in the Schooner Inn, listening out for the town's children going to school.

Under Milk Wood is probably Dylan's best-known work. It was originally written as a 'play for voices' but it wasn't long before it was acted on stage.

It has caught the imagination of many visual artists and inspired sculptures and ceramic wall plaques, as well as textiles and paintings.

The White Horse Tavern, New York, one of Dylan's favourite watering holes

Dylan planned to stay in the New York area. Rehearsals kept him busy but he still found time to visit the clubs and bars of the city where *Under Milk Wood* had been premiered earlier in the year. At each performance the audience gave it a great reception. The play was a masterpiece.

By now Dylan was very ill. He was working much too hard but he was also partying and drinking heavily. On the evening of 4 November 1953 he collapsed and went into a coma. He died five days later at St Vincent's Hospital in New York.

There has always been a mystery about Dylan Thomas's death, and nobody knows exactly what killed him. Perhaps it was a combination of things. He had certainly drunk a lot of whisky. He had suffered from asthma since he was a little boy and the high levels of air pollution in New York might have made it harder for him to breathe. Some people wonder whether he was given the right medical treatment or whether he got it quickly enough.

His body was brought back to Wales and buried in the new churchyard at Laugharne. Many people come to visit Dylan's grave each year.

St Martin's Church, Laugharne

Fern Hill
Dylan Thomas

Now as I was young and easy under the apple boughs
About the lilting house and happy as the grass was green,
    The night above the dingle starry,
      Time let me hail and climb
    Golden in the heydays of his eyes,
And honoured among wagons I was prince of the apple towns
And once below a time I lordly had the trees and leaves
      Trail with daisies and barley
    Down the rivers of the windfall light.

And as I was green and carefree, famous among the barns
About the happy yard and singing as the farm was home,
    In the sun that is young once only,
      Time let me play and be
    Golden in the mercy of his means,
And green and golden I was huntsman and herdsman, the calves
Sang to my horn, the foxes on the hills barked clear and cold,
      And the sabbath rang slowly
    In the pebbles of the holy streams.

All the sun long it was running, it was lovely, the hay
Fields high as the house, the tunes from the chimneys, it was air
    And playing, lovely and watery
      And fire green as grass.
    And nightly under the simple stars
As I rode to sleep the owls were bearing the farm away,
All the moon long I heard, blessed among stables, the nightjars
      Flying with the ricks, and the horses
        Flashing into the dark.

And then to awake, and the farm, like a wanderer white
With the dew, come back, the cock on his shoulder : it was all
    Shining, it was Adam and maiden,
      The sky gathered again
    And the sun grew round that very day.
So it must have been after the birth of the simple light
In the first, spinning place, the spellbound horses walking warm
      Out of the whinnying green stable
        On to the fields of praise.

And honoured among foxes and pheasants by the gay house
Under the new made clouds and happy as the heart was long,
    In the sun born over and over,
      I ran my heedless ways,
    My wishes raced through the house high hay
And nothing I cared, at my sky blue trades, that time allows
In all his tuneful turning so few and such morning songs
      Before the children green and golden
        Follow him out of grace,

Nothing I cared, in the lamb white days, that time would take me
Up to the swallow thronged loft by the shadow of my hand,
    In the moon that is always rising,
      Nor that riding to sleep
    I should hear him fly with the high fields
And wake to the farm forever fled from the childless land.
Oh as I was young and easy in the mercy of his means,
      Time held me green and dying
    Though I sang in my chains like the sea.

There is no doubt that Dylan Thomas was a great writer. But he was plagued with doubts and terrified that his genius would, one day, leave him.

Not everything he wrote was successful. Some of his poetry is complicated and difficult. But in some of his short stories, his magnificent radio broadcasts, and, arguably, in the wonderful poem, 'Fern Hill', he managed to catch and draw his memories of childhood.

That's what makes him a great writer.

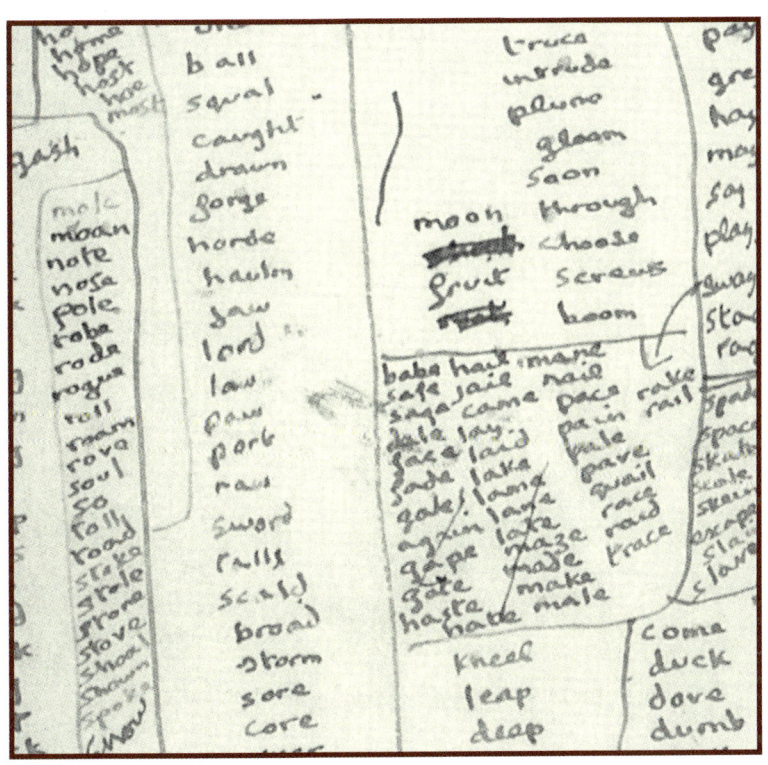

What to Read/Watch

Some of Dylan Thomas's writing is very complicated, especially his poetry, but it's well worth making the effort to sample some of his original work. Here are some good places to start:

Stories and Plays

A Child's Christmas in Wales

Portrait of the Artist as a Young Dog

Under Milk Wood

Poems

'Fern Hill'

'Poem In October'

'Do Not Go Gentle Into That Goodnight'

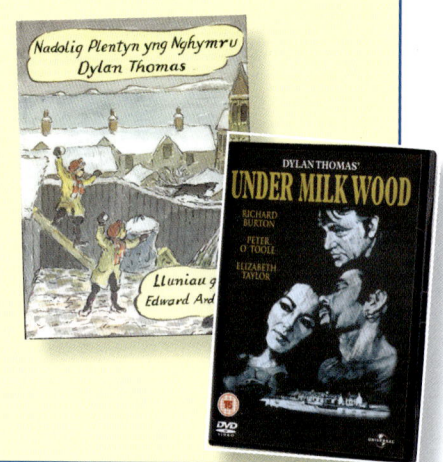

Where to Visit

Dylan's birthplace in Cwmdonkin Drive, Swansea
http://5cwmdonkindrive.com/

Cwmdonkin Park
http://cwmdonkinpark.com/

The Dylan Thomas Centre
http://www.swansea.gov.uk/dtc

The Boathouse at Laugharne
http://www.dylanthomasboathouse.com

What to Do

Make a shoebox collection of memories from when you were younger. You could include photographs, objects, paintings or sketches to help you remember exactly where you were and how you felt. Why not choose a memory to turn into a poem, using a different line for each of your five senses, or, use your set of memories to create a play for voices?